smoothies

louise pickford   *photography by* ian wallace

smoothies

OVER 100 FABULOUS BLENDED DRINKS
FROM BREAKFAST BOOSTERS TO INDULGENT TREATS

RYLAND
PETERS
& SMALL

LONDON NEW YORK

Senior Editor **Clare Double**
Production **Paul Harding**
Art Director **Leslie Harrington**
Publishing Director **Alison Starling**

Stylist **Louise Pickford**
Nutritionist **Anthia Kollouros**

First published in the
United States in 2008
by Ryland Peters & Small
519 Broadway, 5th Floor
New York, NY 10012
www.rylandpeters.com

10 9 8 7 6 5 4 3 2 1

Printed in China

Library of Congress Cataloging-in-Publication Data

Pickford, Louise.
  Smoothies : over 100 fabulous blended drinks
from breakfast boosters to indulgent treats /
Louise Pickford ; photography by Ian Wallace.
       p. cm.
  Includes index.
  ISBN 978-1-84597-594-4
1. Blenders (Cookery) 2. Smoothies
(Beverages)
  I. Title.
  TX840.B5P53 2008
  641.5'893--dc22
                                    2007035947

I would like to thank everyone at RPS for their
continued support, my husband for his beautiful
photography and his thirst for smoothies, and
Alice for her help with testing and blending skills!

Notes

• All spoon measurements are level, unless
otherwise specified.

• All milk is whole (full-fat), unless otherwise
specified.

• All fruit and vegetables are medium-sized,
unless otherwise specified.

• Yogurt is plain, unless otherwise specified.

CONVERSION CHARTS

Volume equivalents:

American	Metric	Imperial
¼ cup	60 ml	2 fl oz.
⅓ cup	75 ml	2½ fl oz.
½ cup	125 ml	4 fl oz.
⅔ cup	150 ml	5 fl oz (¼ pint)
¾ cup	175 ml	6 fl oz.
1 cup	250 ml	8 fl oz.

Weight equivalents:

Imperial	Metric
1 oz.	25 g
2 oz.	55 g
3 oz.	85 g
4 oz.	115 g
5 oz.	140 g
6 oz.	175 g
7 oz.	200 g
8 oz. (½ lb)	225 g
9 oz.	250 g
10 oz.	280 g
11 oz.	325 g
12 oz.	350 g
13 oz.	375 g
14 oz.	400 g
15 oz.	425 g
16 oz. (1 lb.)	450 g
2 lb.	900 g

CONTENTS

INTRODUCTION

A smoothie is the generic name given to a drink made by blending fruits, yogurt, milk, or juice, and often ice, to give a thick, satisfying, and nutritionally balanced drink. This book includes some favorite smoothies as well as other blended drinks and juices to provide a comprehensive collection of recipes for every occasion. So whether you are looking for an energizing morning smoothie, a refreshing afternoon thirst quencher, or even something to calm the nerves or soothe the stomach, then this is the perfect book.

Making smoothies, milkshakes, frappés, and fruit juices couldn't be simpler. All the recipes in this book are made using either a blender or a juicer (sometimes you'll need both). The main difference between blended drinks and juices is that the whole fruit is usually used to make a blended drink, while a juicer extracts the skin, seeds, and pulp of the fruit as part of the juicing process. Both pieces of equipment can be expensive, but there are many cheaper versions available that work perfectly well. Do some research before purchasing to ensure you get the best machine or machines for you.

Blending is really quick and easy; simply pop the ingredients in the blender and process until smooth, transfer to a glass, and drink! Juicers are just as easy to use, but are a little more time-consuming to clean. However, the benefits far outweigh the mess, and freshly made juices are definitely worth it. It's simply a matter of habit: once you start making smoothies or juices at home, you'll never stop. They are that good.

I hope you enjoy making and drinking these juices as much as I did and continue to do so. I still find it hard to believe that something so good for you can taste as delicious as these recipes. Happy blending.

HEALTH BENEFITS

To me, a classic smoothie is an extra-thick drink mainly consumed instead of breakfast, and which provides protein, fiber, and enough energy to keep you going until lunchtime. It can contain foods such as wheat germ, tofu, nuts, and dried fruits, making it thick enough to chew. In fact, chewing your drink has real benefits as the process enhances the production of saliva and digestive enzymes. Fiber, which is essential to keep the gut working smoothly and help promote good intestinal bacteria, is often lacking from Western diets, so smoothies are a sure-fire way of ensuring we get sufficient.

Milk-based blended drinks, or milkshakes, are those icy cold, frothy, fruit-flavored drinks that immediately conjure up pleasant childhood memories. Using fresh fruit instead of a fruit syrup means that they can be healthy as well as delicious. Mostly made using cow's milk, shakes are packed full of calcium, which is essential for healthy bones, teeth, and gums, and hair growth. Calcium also helps prevent the onset of osteoporosis.

Fruit juices or frappés are blends of fruit and ice and are both refreshing and healthy. There are limitless possibilities here, and I have only scratched the surface with my choice of combinations. Juices are an instant health boost, providing us with an immediate hit of nutrients, and many of my juices are designed with specific health benefits in mind. Our bodies are able to absorb the nutrients from juices without having to break down and digest complex foods. Ultimately juices ensure we get the maximum benefit from our fruit with high yields of the minerals, vitamins, and cleansing elements so essential in a healthy diet.

Many people are allergic to or intolerant of cow's milk, are vegan or simply prefer to avoid dairy products, so I have included a whole chapter of dairy-free drinks. The alternatives include soy milk, rice milk, oat milk, sheep's milk, and goat's milk. You can also buy soy, sheep's milk, and goat's milk yogurts. As always when buying processed food, read the labels for hidden additives. Soy milk, rice milk, and oat milk often have sugars or sweeteners, oils, and salt added, and I recommend buying organic milk and yogurt free of genetically modified organisms whenever possible. If you choose soy milk, buy one fortified with calcium, which is destroyed during the processing of soy.

PRACTICALITIES

The recipes are a guideline for you to follow, but feel free to adapt flavors according to your personal preferences. The quantities will yield more or less what the recipes state, but they will vary because it is doubtful that you will buy the exact size fruits or vegetables I did (exact quantities will not affect the overall flavor). I always use a medium-sized fruit or vegetable unless specified in the recipe.

Preparation is important when making juices and smoothies. Use fresh fruits and vegetables whenever you can—the fresher they are, the better. I prefer to use frozen berries unless fresh berries are in season and cheap. Cut up fruit and vegetables just prior to blending or juicing so they do not lose any of their nutrients. If you're juicing, cut the ingredients into pieces that will fit easily through the feeder funnel on your juicer. You will need to use a juicer for all the recipes in the Vegetable Juices chapter, but for many of the other drinks you can substitute ready-made juice for the whole fruit in the recipes. When buying juices, always check the labels as many brands contain artificial sweeteners and preservatives. I prefer to use organic juices when I can.

Serve all drinks immediately for maximum enjoyment, especially juice-based drinks, which may separate on standing, and drinks made with ice or frozen fruit, which should be drunk really chilled.

GLOSSARY

Anthocyanin is the water-soluble pigment found in berries that gives them their blue-red color.

Antioxidants bind to free radicals before they cause harm to the body and are the key to slowing the biological aging process. Free radicals can damage the DNA in cells, leading to cancer, and they can oxidize cholesterol, leading to clogged blood vessels, heart attack, and stroke.

Beta-carotene is the mineral, found in orange or dark green fruits and vegetables, that is responsible for converting vitamin A in the body.

Bioflavonoids and **flavonoids** are pigments found in many fruits and vegetables, including the pith and membrane of citrus fruit. They have antioxidant properties.

Glycemic index The glycemic index ranks foods by the speed at which their carbohydrates are converted to glucose in the body. It measures the effects of foods on blood-sugar levels.

Lactose is the sugar or carbohydrate found in milk, which the body normally breaks down into simpler components

with the help of the enzyme lactase. Without enough lactase, digestion problems can occur. This is known as lactose intolerance.

Lauric acid is the essential fatty acid that makes up more than 50% of the total saturated fats found in coconut milk. It is responsible for building and maintaining the body's immune system. The only other source of lauric acid is mother's milk.

Lecithin is a fatty substance found in some foods including avocado. It is essential for the metabolism of fats in the body.

Organic food is produced without chemical fertilizers or pesticides. I recommend using organic milk and yogurt. It is especially beneficial because it is rich in probiotics, which help digestion, re-establish the good bacteria in the stomach, and strengthen the immune system.

Polyphenol is an antioxidant that helps to prevent or neutralize the damaging effects of free radicals.

Probiotics are microorganisms that help digestion by interacting with the good bacteria in the stomach.

BREAKFAST SMOOTHIES

Smoothies can make a complete meal and contain a good balance of nutrients including protein, carbohydrates for energy, and fiber. As the first meal of the day is such an important one, smoothies provide the perfect start. They are tasty, highly nutritious, and quick and easy to prepare. The variations are endless, as you will see from some of the delicious combinations in this chapter.

BLUEBERRY MUESLI SMOOTHIE

8 oz. fresh or frozen
blueberries

1 cup organic yogurt

1 cup organic milk

⅓ cup muesli

**1 teaspoon pure vanilla
extract**

SERVES: 2

BLUEBERRY MUESLI SMOOTHIE

This smoothie is a meal in a glass; it is easily to digest and perfect for a busy morning when you need breakfast on the run. To enhance absorption of the nutrients, chew the liquid to stimulate the production of saliva and digestive enzymes.

Put all the ingredients in a blender and blend until smooth.

Blueberries are rich in antioxidants called anthocyanins. Anthocyanins are the pigments found in blue-red fruits and vegetables. They help strengthen capillaries, are good for eye health, and have antiaging properties. Blueberries are also a great fruit for diabetics and those with candida, as they are low in sugar.

1 mango

1 banana

1 ¼ cups tropical fruit juice

1 cup organic yogurt

**2 tablespoons blanched
almonds**

SERVES: 2

TROPICAL FRUIT BOOSTER

Here the usual milk is replaced with a mixed fruit juice, giving this drink a fantastic tropical flavor and a lighter taste. Bananas not only add bulk to a drink; they are also a terrific source of fiber and carbohydrate and a vital source of energy.

Prepare the mango by slicing down each side of the pit and cutting away the flesh from the skin. Dice the flesh into a blender. Peel and slice the banana and add to the mango with the fruit juice, yogurt, and almonds. Blend until smooth.

Almonds are a rich source of vitamin E, an antioxidant and skin healer, and contain monounsaturated fat, which is good for lowering cholesterol. They also provide a good source of fiber.

¼ cup dried apricots

1 cup pear juice

**1 tablespoon blanched
almonds**

1 tablespoon sunflower seeds

1 ½ cups organic milk

1 cup organic yogurt

SERVES: 2–3

APRICOT ENERGIZER

Using dried fruits in smoothies boosts energy levels as they are rich in the fruit sugars fructose and glucose. The almonds and sunflower seeds provide minerals as well as good monounsaturated fats, which balance the sugars and sustain and maintain the energy from the apricots over a longer period of time. Make sure you use preservative-free dried apricots.

Put the apricots and pear juice in a small saucepan, heat gently to boiling, cover, and simmer gently for 5 minutes until softened. Set aside to cool completely.

Put the apricots and juice in a blender with the remaining ingredients and blend until smooth.

PAPAYA, MELON, and PEAR DIGESTIVE

PAPAYA, MELON, and PEAR DIGESTIVE

A native of Asia, ginger has both culinary and medicinal values—its distinctive tang adds a wonderful flavor and "kick" to foods, while healing properties include aiding digestion, preventing the formation of blood clots, and even reducing cholesterol levels. Papaya also aids digestion, and the melon is both cooling and hydrating. Take this drink without food, as melon tends to ferment some foods in the stomach and can cause bloating.

I small papaya, about 12 oz.

2 cups cantaloupe pieces

I cup pear juice

freshly squeezed juice of I large lime

I teaspoon grated fresh ginger

SERVES: 2

Peel the papaya and cut it in half, scoop out and discard the seeds, and then chop the flesh. Put the papaya and cantaloupe pieces in a blender and add the remaining ingredients. Blend until smooth.

GYM JUNKIE

2 bananas

¼ cup wheat germ

I cup pear juice

½ cup sheep's milk yogurt

4 oz. silken tofu

2 tablespoons pecans

I tablespoon sunflower seeds

SERVES: 2

If you're an early-bird gym user, then drink this power-packed smoothie before you go. Banana is rich in potassium, a blood pressure and fluid regulator, and will provide vital carbohydrate energy before your workout.

Peel and slice the bananas and put in a blender with the remaining ingredients. Blend until smooth.

Wheat germ contains vitamin E, some B vitamins, and zinc and is believed to improve colon function, nourish the skin, lower cholesterol, and boost the immune system. Best stored in the fridge once opened to retain its properties. Not tolerable by gluten-sensitive people or those suffering from celiac disease.

BANANA, PRUNE, and GRANOLA CRUNCH

If you're not a prune fan then this delicious drink will be a pleasant surprise, allowing you to make the most of the prunes' bowel-cleansing properties while enjoying the creamy flavor and nutty texture of the bananas and granola. Cinnamon aids digestion and adds a deliciously warming spicy flavor.

6 pitted prunes (dried plums), preferably preservative free

I cup apple juice

I banana

⅓ cup granola

¼ teaspoon ground cinnamon, plus extra for dusting

I cup sheep's milk

5 oz. sheep's milk yogurt

SERVES: 2

Put the prunes and apple juice in a small saucepan and bring to a boil, then cover and simmer gently for 5 minutes until softened. Remove from the heat and set aside to cool completely.

Peel and slice the banana. Put in a blender with the prune mixture, granola, cinnamon, milk, and yogurt and blend until smooth. Serve dusted with a little extra cinnamon.

Sheep's milk and sheep's milk yogurt are richer in nutrients such as calcium and magnesium, and easier to digest, than cow's milk products.

LEFT TO RIGHT **WATERMELON and RASPBERRY SURPRISE, MORNING CLEANSER, BANANARAMA**

BANANARAMA

2 large bananas

1¼ cups buttermilk

1 tablespoon honey

SERVES: 2

This is another energy drink best consumed before aerobic activity. Bananas provide an instant and sustained energy boost, which is why we often see sports people eating them during a game. In fact just two bananas will provide the body with enough energy for a 90-minute workout!

Peel and slice the bananas and put in a blender with the buttermilk and honey. Blend until smooth.

Bananas are a rich source of potassium, which is important for enzyme production, regulating the water balance in the body and blood pressure, and nerve and muscle function. Bananas also help lubricate the intestines and lungs.

WATERMELON and RASPBERRY SURPRISE

large wedge watermelon, about 2¼ lbs.

5 oz. fresh or frozen raspberries

1 tablespoon rosewater

SERVES: 3

The surprise here is the curious yet exotic flavor of rosewater—it's quite intriguing. This is a particularly refreshing morning drink that satisfies the senses as well as the stomach. Watermelon is both cooling and hydrating, while rosewater is uplifting, a stress reliever, and soothes the nerves.

Cut the watermelon into chunks. Put in a blender with the raspberries and rosewater and blend until smooth.

MORNING CLEANSER

4 firm ripe pears, about 22 oz.

½ cucumber

1 small grapefruit

2-inch piece fresh ginger

SERVES: 2

Mornings are not always about get-up-and-go and we often feel the need to detox, especially after a late night of over-indulgence! Pears are very cleansing and cucumber is about the best diuretic around—this combination is perfect for cleaning the system. With the addition of grapefruit, which aids in overcoming alcohol intoxication, you can say goodbye to your hangover. The ginger awakens the senses through smell and taste.

Cut the pears and cucumber into chunks. Peel the grapefruit and cut into wedges. Press everything through a juicer into a pitcher.

Pear is cooling and hydrating, excellent after an evening involving drinking, excess heat, and dehydration. Pears are also rich in fibers that can bind to toxins and help remove them from the body.

KICK START YOUR DAY

This is a lovely drink to start your day—freshly ground flaxseed helps lubricate the skin and reduce inflammation, and it is also rich in fiber. Tahini is a rich source of calcium, important for healthy teeth, bones, and hair, and contains good fats, which also help nourish the skin.

Crush the flaxseed using a pestle and mortar or spice grinder. To prepare the mango, slice down each side of the pit and cut away the flesh from the skin. Peel and slice the banana. Put the fruit in a blender with the ground flaxseed, oat bran, and tahini and blend for 30 seconds. Add the yogurt and milk and blend until smooth.

Oat bran is an excellent source of soluble fiber, which helps promote easy bowel movements. It should be avoided by those with gluten sensitivities. Replace the oat bran with a tablespoon of sunflower seeds, if preferred.

I tablespoon flaxseed
I small mango, about 14 oz.
I banana
2 tablespoons oat bran
I tablespoon tahini
I cup sheep's milk yogurt
I cup sheep's milk

SERVES: 2

AVOCADO, PEAR, and MINT COOLER

Unlike most fruit, avocado has a high fat content, but it is monounsaturated fat, so will not raise cholesterol levels. Avocados are also rich in lecithin and minerals, making them great brain food. The addition of mint adds a refreshing quality to the drink, and this aromatic herb also calms the digestive tract and helps quell nausea.

Cut the avocado in half and remove the seed. Scoop out the flesh and put in a blender with the pear juice, mint, and lime juice and blend until smooth.

I avocado
2¼ cups pear juice
leaves from 4 mint sprigs
freshly squeezed juice
of I lime

SERVES: 2–3

APRICOT, BANANA, and BRAZIL NUT SMOOTHIE

Brazil nuts contain the essential trace mineral selenium, which acts as a powerful antioxidant to help guard against some degenerative diseases such as cancer and heart disease. Maple syrup is a great alternative to sugar and honey as it is rich in minerals, enhancing the absorption of selenium.

Peel and slice the banana. Cut the apricots in half and remove the pits. Put the fruit in a blender with the remaining ingredients and blend until smooth.

Apricots are rich in beta-carotene and iron and are good for eye health and combating anemia.

I banana
4 fresh apricots
I cup organic yogurt
I cup apricot nectar
I tablespoon pure maple syrup
3 tablespoons Brazil nuts

SERVES: 2

LEFT **KICK START YOUR DAY**

RIGHT **AVOCADO, PEAR, and MINT COOLER**

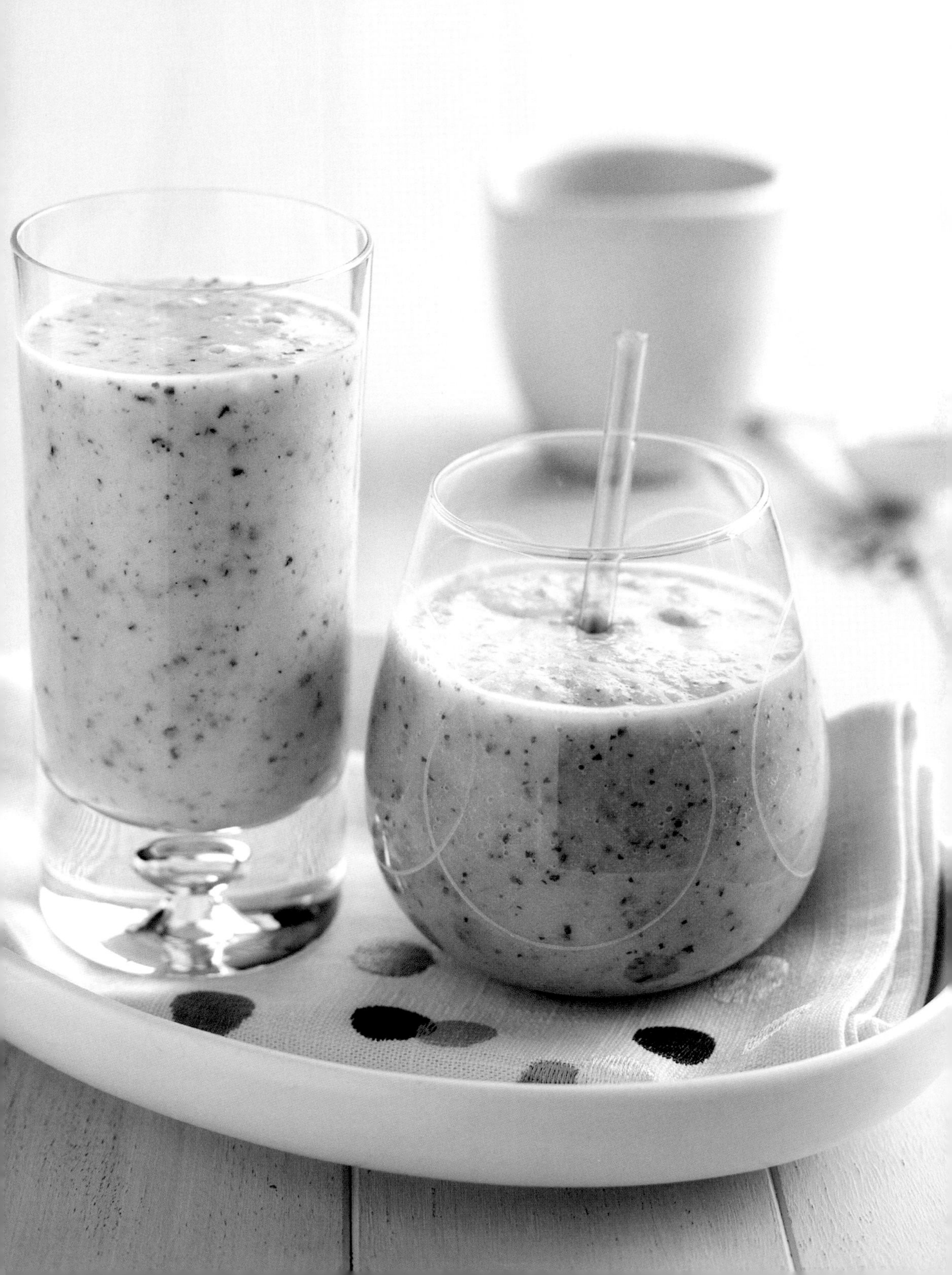

VITAMIN C BOOST JUICE

MOCHA PROTEIN DRINK

Designer protein powders are increasingly popular with athletes and keep-fit fanatics as they are easy to add to drinks, giving an instant energy boost. Available from health-food stores, they come in several flavors including chocolate. If you don't want to buy a protein powder, use organic cocoa powder instead.

Peel and slice the banana. Dissolve the coffee granules in the water. Put all the ingredients in a blender and process until smooth.

1 banana

2 teaspoons organic coffee granules

3 tablespoons boiling water

1¼ cups organic milk

1 tablespoon chocolate protein powder

4 scoops vanilla soy ice cream

SERVES: 2

VITAMIN C BOOST JUICE

All three fruits here are a valuable source of vitamin C, so this tangy juice is perfect for an early morning boost. Vitamin C aids against gum disease, helps protect our bodies from cancer, heart disease, colds, and flu, and helps reduce stress. It is even believed to delay the aging process, as it promotes healthy skin.

Peel and chop the oranges and grapefruit, leaving some of the pith intact (see note below). Hull the strawberries and press all the fruit through a juicer into a pitcher. Serve poured over ice.

The white pith on citrus fruits is high in antioxidants and I recommend that it is included in the juice for its health benefits.

6 oranges

3 ruby grapefruit

3 cups strawberries

ice cubes, to serve

SERVES: 3–4

DAIRY-FREE BREAKFAST SMOOTHIE

This delicious drink will definitely give you a boost of energy with its high-sugar fruit, but it also provides natural vitamins, minerals, and fiber to sustain your energy levels until lunchtime.

Peel and slice the banana. To prepare the mango, slice down each side of the pit and cut away the flesh from the skin. Put the banana and mango in a blender with the blueberries, muesli, and apple juice. Blend until smooth.

1 banana

1 small mango, about 14 oz.

1 cup fresh or frozen blueberries

⅓ cup muesli

2¼ cups apple juice

SERVES: 3

FRUIT FRAPPÉS

A frappé is an iced drink made with fresh fruits plus ice, frozen fruits, or fruit sorbets, blended together and drunk well chilled. You can blend any mixture of fruits, but I wanted to include some of my favorite combinations as well as those designed to give you an instant boost of energy, vitality, and nutritional benefits. I recommend using frozen berries for the recipes in this chapter as the drinks are best when really cold, but fresh fruits and ice are just as good. Serve frappés immediately, before they warm up.

BERRY BLITZ

With all these wonderful berries this is an antioxidant power drink—it is antiaging, great for healthy eye function, capillary strength, and combating varicose veins.

Put all the ingredients in a blender and blend until smooth.

¾ cup frozen raspberries
¾ cup frozen strawberries
¾ cup frozen blueberries
2¼ cups apple juice

SERVES: 2

WATERMELON WHIZZ

Hydrate, hydrate, and hydrate with this drink! This one is best drunk on an empty stomach when you won't be eating for a while, as watermelon can ferment some foods and cause bloating.

Roughly chop the watermelon flesh away from the skin, put in a blender with the lime juice and ice, and blend until smooth.

Lime is cooling, antiseptic, and aids the absorption of nutrients.

large wedge watermelon, about 3½ lbs.
freshly squeezed juice of 1 lime
12 ice cubes

SERVES: 3–4

CARIBBEAN CRUSH

Consume this delicious tropical-inspired drink half an hour before a meal to aid digestion.

Peel the pineapple and discard the thick central core. Cut the flesh into chunks. To prepare the mango, slice down each side of the pit and cut away the flesh from the skin. Put the mango and pineapple in a blender. Cut the passion fruit in half and scoop the pulp into the blender, add the ice, and blend until smooth.

Mango is a rich source of vitamin A and is also good for eye and skin health.

½ pineapple
1 mango
2 ripe passion fruit
8 ice cubes

SERVES: 2

FROZEN BERRY and BANANA BLEND

This naturally sweet blend of fruits is rich in vitamin C —it will bring a smile to your face and balance to both your immune system and your bowels!

Peel and slice the banana. Put all the ingredients in a blender and blend until smooth.

1 banana
1½ cups frozen mixed berries
1 cup apple juice
2 scoops berry sorbet

SERVES: 2

FRUIT BOWL FRAPPÉ

A lovely balance of vitamin C-rich flavors. Include some of the white orange pith as it contains not only fiber but bioflavonoids, which enhance the absorption of vitamin C found in the juice. If you don't have a juicer, use ½ cup each of organic apple and orange juice instead of the whole fruits.

Quarter the apples and cut in half again if large. Peel the oranges, leaving some of the pith intact, and cut the flesh into chunks. Press the apples and oranges through a juicer into a pitcher.

Peel and slice the banana. Put in a blender with the apple and orange juice, strawberries, and ice cubes and blend until smooth.

2 apples
2 oranges
1 banana
2 cups frozen strawberries
8 ice cubes

SERVES: 2

BLUEBERRY BUZZ

The blueberries and cranberry juice combine to great effect in this refreshing drink. It is simple but delicious and nutritious, especially if you use organic, sugar-free cranberry juice, available from good health-food stores.

Put the blueberries and cranberry juice in a blender and blend until smooth.

Cranberries are a rich source of polyphenol antioxidants, chemicals that are known to benefit the cardiovascular and immune systems. They are also traditionally used for the treatment of cystitis.

8 oz. frozen blueberries
1 cup cranberry juice

SERVES: 2

LEFT TO RIGHT

FROZEN BERRY and BANANA BLEND

FRUIT BOWL FRAPPÉ

BLUEBERRY BUZZ

PEACH, APRICOT, and PLUM FIZZ

These delicious stone fruits are at their best when bought in season for their aromatic and nutritional qualities. They are rich in antioxidants and vitamin C, especially when combined with orange juice. A great drink to aid against anemia and ward off colds and flu.

Halve the peach, plum, and apricots and discard the pits. Roughly chop the flesh, put in a blender with the orange juice and ice, and blend until really smooth.

1 peach
1 plum
2 fresh apricots
½ cup freshly squeezed orange juice
8 ice cubes

SERVES: 2

AUTUMN CLASSIC

This adaptable drink is delicious served cooled with ice or as a virgin mulled wine—warm it over a low heat (without the ice cubes) for a nourishing and sustaining drink, especially if the autumn nights are starting to feel chilly.

Cut the apples into pieces and press through a juicer into a pitcher. Pour the juice into a blender and add the remaining ingredients. Blend until smooth.

4 apples
2½ cups frozen blackberries
1 tablespoon pure maple syrup or brown sugar
a pinch of ground cinnamon
6 ice cubes

SERVES: 2–3

PINEAPPLE, GINGER, and MINT SLUSHIE

This fruit concoction is an excellent digestive aid best drunk half an hour before you eat or as a refreshing, cooling drink on a hot summer's day. It is excellent for morning sickness in pregnancy or any time when feeling nauseous.

Peel the pineapple and remove the tough central core. Roughly chop the flesh and put in a blender with the ginger, mint, and ice. Blend until really smooth.

Ginger helps break down undigested food and quell nausea. It promotes circulation, and when added to a drink can help carry the other ingredients through the body.

½ small pineapple, about 18 oz.
1 teaspoon grated fresh ginger
leaves from 2 mint sprigs
8 ice cubes

SERVES: 2

LEFT PINEAPPLE, GINGER, and MINT SLUSHIE

RIGHT PEACH, APRICOT, and PLUM FIZZ

MELON, CUCUMBER, and SWEET GINGER FRAPPÉ

½ **Galia melon, about 2 lb.**

½ **cucumber**

**freshly squeezed juice
of ½ lime**

**1 tablespoon chopped
stem ginger**

**1 tablespoon ginger syrup
from the jar**

6 ice cubes

SERVES: 2

MELON, CUCUMBER,
and SWEET GINGER FRAPPÉ

The melon, cucumber, and lime make this a hydrating and detoxifying drink. It has an added kick of spicy ginger to increase circulation. Ginger in any form is a great remedy for nausea.

Seed the melon and scoop the flesh into a blender. Peel and chop the cucumber and add to the blender with the remaining ingredients. Blend until smooth.

Melon is cooling and hydrating and is rich in minerals—this is a further hydration aid, as minerals carry water into the body's cells.

2 pears

2 oranges

1 banana

8 ice cubes

SERVES: 2

ORANGE, PEAR,
and BANANA BREEZE

There's plenty of fiber, vitamin C, and energy in this lovely drink. If you're in a hurry, substitute 1 cup each of pear and orange juice for the whole fruits and make this drink using just a blender.

Cut the pears into chunks. Peel the oranges and cut the flesh into pieces. Press the pear and orange pieces through a juicer into a pitcher and then pour the juice into a blender. Peel and slice the banana and add it to the blender with the ice cubes. Blend until smooth.

LEFT TO RIGHT

FROZEN CRANBERRY, RASPBERRY, and GRAPEFRUIT SLUSHIE

GUAVA, STRAWBERRY, and APPLE REFRESHER

MANGO and STRAWBERRY DELIGHT

GUAVA, STRAWBERRY, and APPLE REFRESHER

Guava is richer in vitamin C than most citrus fruits and is also packed with vitamins A and B. If you like you can make this drink without using a blender, by crushing the ice cubes by hand with an ice crusher, or putting them in a plastic bag and bashing them with a rolling pin. Then mix the juices with the crushed ice.

4 apples
2 cups strawberries
¾ cup guava nectar
12 ice cubes

SERVES: 2–3

Cut the apples into chunks and hull the strawberries. Press the apple pieces and strawberries through a juicer into a pitcher. Pour the juice into a blender and add the guava nectar and ice. Blend until smooth.

FROZEN CRANBERRY, RASPBERRY, and GRAPEFRUIT SLUSHIE

This is a detox tonic, as grapefruit juice significantly increases the production and activity of liver detoxification enzymes. For extra bioflavonoid activity keep the pith on the grapefruit to aid vitamin C absorption. If you don't want to use a juicer, substitute 1¼ cups freshly squeezed grapefruit juice for the whole grapefruit.

3 ruby grapefruit
1¼ cups cranberry juice
4 scoops raspberry sorbet

SERVES: 2

Peel the grapefruit, retaining some of the pith, cut the flesh into chunks, and press through a juicer. Pour into a blender, add the cranberry juice and sorbet and blend until smooth. Transfer to a shallow plastic container and freeze for 4 hours. Return to the blender and process to form a slushie.

MANGO and STRAWBERRY DELIGHT

Mangoes at their best are a true gift of nature. It's just a shame that they are often picked underripe and we rarely get to eat them at their peak—unless you are lucky enough to have a mango tree in your garden! When choosing mangoes, squeeze them lightly; they should yield a little without feeling squishy and should have a fragrant, even heady aroma. If available buy the Alphonso mango (from India): it is magnificent. This frappé calls for fresh rather than frozen strawberries to complement the wonderfully sweet flavor of the mango.

2 mangoes
2 cups strawberries
ice cubes, to serve

SERVES: 2

Cut down each side of the mango pit and scoop the flesh into a blender. Hull the strawberries, add to the mango, and blend until smooth. Serve over ice.

RASPBERRY and APPLE FIZZ

2⅓ cups frozen raspberries
1 cup apple juice
12 ice cubes
sparkling water, to serve

SERVES: 4

This is a truly refreshing drink for a hot summer's day, and with the addition of the sparkling water it makes a delightful non-alcoholic cocktail.

Put the raspberries, apple juice, and ice in a blender and blend until smooth. Pour into 4 tall glasses and top up with sparkling water.

Raspberries are packed with fiber, antioxidants, and other beneficial phytochemicals, which have disease-preventative properties.

MANGO, RASPBERRY, and CRANBERRY CRUISE

1 large mango, about 18 oz.
1¼ cups frozen raspberries
1 cup cranberry juice
1 teaspoon honey, to taste

SERVES: 2

A perfectly ripe mango is aromatic, with an ambrosial flavor and creamy-smooth silky texture. Combined with raspberries and a cranberry juice base, mango makes a perfect replenishing energy drink after strenuous exercise.

Cut down each side of the mango pit and dice the flesh into a blender. Add the raspberries and cranberry juice and blend until smooth. Taste and add a teaspoon of honey to sweeten, if necessary.

RASPBERRY and APPLE FIZZ

VEGETABLE JUICES

I always thought of vegetable juices as a bit "hard core" and for the health fanatic only, but I was more than pleasantly surprised by just how delicious and varied the flavors were when I was developing these drinks. Not only are they packed with goodness and taste fantastic, but some will even help ward off colds and chase away the effects of a hangover! Although you can serve vegetable juices at any time of day, I found that most were particularly invigorating as morning drinks, a good way to cleanse both the body and soul.

LEFT **AUTUMN CRUMBLE**

RIGHT **GINGER SPICE**

1 apple

1 pear

1 large carrot, about 7 oz.

1 fennel bulb, about 6 oz., trimmed

½-inch piece fresh ginger

SERVES: 1

AUTUMN CRUMBLE

This is a health tonic that promotes regular bowel movements and the elimination of mucus. Ginger helps eliminate mucus from the sinuses and acts as a digestive, so this drink is both stimulating and calming.

Cut the apple, pear, carrot, and fennel into chunks that will fit into the funnel on your juicer. Press all the ingredients through the juicer into a large glass.

Fennel helps eliminate liver stagnancy and acts as a digestive.

2 oranges

1 beet, about 5 oz., trimmed and scrubbed

2 carrots

SERVES: 1–2

GENTLE SUNRISE JUICE

Rich in vitamins and colorful antioxidant pigments, this drink will rejuvenate you, delaying the aging process. A sweet pick-me-up that will bring a healthy glow to your cheeks.

Peel the oranges and cut the flesh into chunks. Cut the beet and carrots into chunks and press everything through a juicer into a pitcher.

Carrots are a good source of beta-carotene and enhance the elimination of toxins.

½ lemon

1 fennel bulb, about 6 oz., trimmed

1 apple

1-inch piece fresh ginger

¾ cup green grapes

SERVES: 3

GINGER SPICE

This lip-smacking juice is a potent digestive aid. It will help purge the bowels and clear the sinuses. Best served in shot glasses for an instant kick-start to your day.

Peel the lemon, discarding the white pith, and cut into chunks. Cut the fennel and apple into smallish chunks and then press all the ingredients through a juicer into a pitcher.

2 carrots

2 oranges

1 pomegranate, about 12 oz.

a few drops of rosewater

SERVES: 1–2

MIDDLE EASTERN DELIGHT

This wonderful rose-colored juice is an immune-system tonic. Traditionally the juices of carrots, oranges, and pomegranates were used as a preventative against cancer, due to their high antioxidant content.

Cut the carrots into chunks. Peel the oranges and cut the flesh into chunks. Press the oranges and carrots through a juicer into a pitcher.

Cut the pomegranate in half. Using a citrus squeezer, extract as much juice as possible. Strain through a sieve into the pitcher. Add the rosewater and stir well.

Pomegranates are ancient fruits native to the Middle East. They are a great source of potassium, and pomegranate juice contains antioxidants that help to protect your blood lipids from oxidization. Pomegranate juice may also help to prevent prostate cancer. The seeds appear to enhance immune function.

2 small ripe tomatoes, about 6 oz.

4½ oz. cucumber

2 celery ribs, trimmed

½ red pepper, cored and seeded

½ lemongrass stalk

½ long red chile, cored and seeded

wedge of cucumber or celery rib, to serve

SERVES: 1

HANGOVER CURE

This nutrient-rich juice is a true pick-me-up, and will help revitalize, hydrate, nourish, and cleanse. Tomatoes can help protect against cancer, while cucumber helps hydrate the body, especially to counteract the effects of alcohol. Lemongrass aids digestion and soothes nausea.

Cut everything into chunks and press through a juicer into a large glass. Serve immediately with a long wedge of cucumber or half a celery rib.

Red pepper is rich in vitamin C and replenishes nutrients lost after a night of drinking.

BREAKFAST ZINGER

1 lemon

1 beet, about 5 oz., trimmed and scrubbed

1 carrot

1 apple

SERVES: 1

This tangy juice is a morning bladder cleanser. Lemons cleanse and aid digestion of the other vegetables. Beta-carotene-rich carrot eliminates toxins, while the apple adds fiber and sweetness.

Peel the lemon, discarding the white pith, and cut into chunks. Cut the vegetables and apple into chunks that will easily fit into the funnel on your juicer and press everything through into a large glass.

Beets have many health benefits. They contain soluble fiber, which helps reduce high blood cholesterol levels, and have an extremely low glycemic index, which means they help keep blood sugar levels stable. Beets are virtually fat free and low in calories.

LEFT **HANGOVER CURE**

CENTER **BREAKFAST ZINGER**

RIIGHT **MIDDLE EASTERN DELIGHT**

1 orange

1 carrot

½ red bell pepper, cored and seeded

½ green bell pepper, cored and seeded

1 celery rib, trimmed

4 oz. cucumber

1½-inch piece fresh ginger

1 ripe tomato

SERVES: 2

SEVENTH HEAVEN

This delicious veggie juice is an A–Z of vitamins and minerals in a glass. Nutrient absorption is aided by the inclusion of ginger, and green and red bell peppers increase circulation and improve vision. This is a perfect drink for the elderly or ill, in whom digestion may be weak and diet poor.

Peel the orange and cut the flesh into chunks. Cut all the remaining ingredients into chunks and then press everything through a juicer into a pitcher.

½ lemon

small wedge honeydew melon, about 6 oz.

½ cucumber

1 celery rib

¾ cup green grapes

a handful of mint leaves

SERVES: 1

WAKE UP and GO JUICE

A potent hydrator and thirst quencher, the cooling cucumber and refreshing mint stimulate the palate and help rid the digestive system of toxins. The naturally rich sugars found in melon and grapes will provide you with a burst of energy.

Peel the lemon, discarding the white pith, and cut into chunks. Cut the melon flesh, cucumber, and celery into chunks. Press all the ingredients through a juicer into a large glass.

Cucumber is an excellent diuretic, and being rich in silicon is beneficial for hair, skin, and nails.

1 small red bell pepper, about 6½ oz., cored and seeded

1 small ripe tomato

4 radishes

1 beet, about 5 oz., trimmed and scrubbed

1 carrot

1 red chile, cored and seeded if wished

2 handfuls arugula or watercress

SERVES: 2

RED ROCKET

Longtime gardeners call arugula "rocket," and while this vibrant juice isn't exactly rocket powered, it will add fire to your belly. It is perfect for those who feel the cold, as it helps stimulate the circulation. Radishes were traditionally prescribed for sufferers of hay fever and sinus congestion. Avoid this drink if you suffer from excess stomach acid.

Cut all the ingredients except the arugula into chunks small enough to fit through the funnel on your juicer. Press everything including the arugula through the juicer into a pitcher.

GREEN GIANT

This juice is green, green, green—the green pigment found in these fruits and vegetables, chlorophyll, provides a welcome balance of alkalinity to an over-acidic state. It also helps deodorize bad breath and body odor, counteracts toxins, is anti-inflammatory, and improves liver function.

2 kiwi fruit

2 pears

4-oz. wedge white cabbage

3½ oz. sugar snap peas

3½ oz. spinach

a small handful of mint leaves

SERVES: 2

Cut the kiwi fruit, pears, and cabbage into pieces that will fit through the funnel on your juicer. Press all the ingredients through the juicer into a pitcher.

Cabbage is excellent for bowel infections such as parasites and inflammation and was traditionally used to counteract stomach and bowel cancers.

SALAD IN A GLASS

A vegetable cocktail that is a valuable source of vitamins, minerals, and antioxidants, especially when you've had to skip a meal or when you need extra nutrients, for example during an illness or period of stress, or after surgery or dental work.

2 small oranges, about 12 oz.

7 oz. romaine or butter lettuce

1 green bell pepper, cored and seeded

2 green apples

4 oz. cucumber

½ bunch of parsley leaves

SERVES: 3

Peel the oranges and cut the flesh into smallish chunks. Cut the lettuce, bell pepper, apples, and cucumber into pieces small enough to fit through the funnel on your juicer. Press all the ingredients through the juicer into a pitcher.

Lettuce contains a natural sedative called lactucarium, and magnesium, which helps calm the nervous system.

CELERY, CARROT, and PINEAPPLE REFRESHER

This fruit and vegetable juice is the perfect digestive aid to drink half an hour before you eat. It is a good anti-nausea remedy in cases of pregnancy, travel sickness, or vertigo. Ginger and peppermint help a fever, while pineapple acts as an anti-inflammatory in fever, sinusitis, and arthritis.

½ small pineapple, about 18 oz.

3 celery ribs, trimmed

2 carrots

a small piece of fresh ginger

leaves from 2 mint sprigs

ice cubes, to serve

SERVES: 2

Peel the pineapple, remove the tough central core, and cut the flesh into chunks. Cut the celery ribs and carrots into chunks. Press all the ingredients through a juicer into a pitcher and serve over ice.

CELERY, CARROT, and
PINEAPPLE REFRESHER

1 orange

2 carrots

8 canned apricot halves in natural juice, drained

1 small garlic clove, crushed

1 teaspoon honey

½ cup crushed ice

SERVES: 2

COLD CURE

This orange drink is a powerful healing tonic. It is a highly absorbable source of vitamins C and A, needed to boost your immune system, combat a cold, and nourish when appetite is low. Try using Manuka honey for an extra potent source of antibacterial effects.

Peel the orange and cut into pieces small enough to fit through the funnel on your juicer. Cut the carrots into similar-sized pieces. Press the orange and carrots through the juicer into a pitcher, then transfer to a blender. Add the apricots, garlic, honey, and ice and blend until smooth.

2 beets, about 10 oz., trimmed and scrubbed

1¼ cups frozen blackberries

1 cup cranberry juice

SERVES: 2–3

DARK SURPRISE

This wonderful juice is called Dark Surprise due to its fantastic deep purple color, from the beets and blackberries. Don't be deterred by this unusual combination; it is truly delicious, sweet and very refreshing, and is also an excellent remedy for cystitis.

Cut the beets into chunks small enough to fit through the funnel on your juicer, then press through into a pitcher. Transfer to a blender, add the blackberries and cranberry juice, and blend until smooth.

½ cucumber

2 green apples

2 cups green grapes

2 sprigs of fresh basil

SERVES: 2

CUCUMBER, GRAPE, and BASIL JUICE

Cucumber is hydrating and cooling, while green grapes will give you an energy boost. Basil was traditionally used to reduce flatulence.

Cut the cucumber and apples into smallish chunks and press through a juicer into a pitcher. Transfer to a blender, add the grapes and basil, and blend until smooth.

DAIRY SMOOTHIES
and SHAKES

Although smoothies are a relatively recent invention, milkshakes seem to have been around forever. In summertime as a kid, I'd often rush home and make myself an instant fruit-flavored shake (not necessarily all that healthy), and trips to the seaside just weren't the same unless we visited a shake bar. This chapter is packed full of old favorites and new inventions, with something for everyone. All are best served well chilled.

MALTED MILO SHAKE

2 cups ripe strawberries

I ripe banana

4 scoops strawberry ice cream, plus extra to serve (optional)

1¼ cups organic milk

SERVES: 2

STRAWBERRY and BANANA SHAKE

This is a perfect chilled summer shake made when strawberries are at their best—choose really ripe fruit with a heady aroma. When strawberries are out of season, use frozen ones instead. Use ice cream flavored with real fruit if possible.

Hull the strawberries and peel and slice the banana. Put the strawberries, banana, ice cream, and milk in a blender and blend until really smooth. Pour into tall glasses and serve topped with extra ice cream, if you like.

2 bananas

4 scoops chocolate ice cream, plus extra to serve (optional)

2 cups organic milk

I teaspoon ground cinnamon

SERVES: 2–3

CHOCOLATE, CINNAMON, and BANANA SMOOTHIE

This smoothie is a firm favorite of kids and grownups alike. Aromatic cinnamon is a perfect match for chocolate and banana, as it aids digestion of both foods. As an extra bonus for adults, cinnamon and chocolate combined were traditionally thought to be an aphrodisiac!

Peel and slice the bananas. Put all the ingredients in a blender and blend until smooth. Pour into glasses and serve topped with an extra scoop of ice cream, if you like.

2 tablespoons Milo (chocolate malt) powder, plus extra for sprinkling

2½ cups organic milk

4 scoops vanilla ice cream

SERVES: 2–3

MALTED MILO SHAKE

Milo powder is a chocolate-flavored food supplement drink, available from supermarkets. It makes great shakes and other drinks. It contains essential minerals and vitamins and has a low glycemic index. If you can't find Milo, use sweetened cocoa mix as an alternative.

Put all the ingredients in a blender and blend until smooth. Pour into glasses and serve sprinkled with extra Milo powder.

PAPAYA, BANANA, and LEMON-LIME SMOOTHIE

½ papaya

1 banana

freshly squeezed juice of ½ lime

2 scoops lemon or lime sorbet

2 cups organic milk

SERVES: 2–3

A refreshing, tangy shake made with sorbet rather than ice cream for a healthier option. I like to use a mixture of lemon and lime sorbets, but you could use just lemon or lime. All variations taste great.

Peel the papaya and scoop out and discard the seeds. Chop the flesh and put it in a blender. Peel and slice the banana, add to the blender with the lime juice, sorbet, and milk and blend until smooth.

CARDAMOM, COFFEE, and DATE SHAKE

4 Medjool dates, pitted

1¼ cups organic milk

½ cup cold espresso coffee

2 scoops vanilla ice cream

½–1 teaspoon ground cardamom, plus extra for sprinkling

SERVES: 2

The addition of dates and ground cardamom gives this iced coffee drink a definite Middle Eastern flavor —a real hint of the exotic. Cardamom improves digestion and provides a heady aroma known to act as an aphrodisiac. Dates and coffee create energy and enhance vitality and libido when combined, so perhaps this is the perfect drink for lovers!

Put the dates in a saucepan with half the milk and heat very gently until the milk just reaches boiling point. Remove the pan from the heat and let cool completely.

When cold, transfer the dates and milk to a blender and add the remaining milk, cold coffee, ice cream, and cardamom. Blend until smooth. Pour into glasses and serve sprinkled with extra ground cardamom.

VANILLA SUPREME

1 vanilla bean

4 scoops vanilla ice cream or sorbet

2 cups organic milk

SERVES: 2

Vanilla adds a smooth texture to the milk and is reminiscent of old-fashioned milkshakes. The spice is also naturally mood-enhancing.

Cut the vanilla bean in half lengthwise and scrape the seeds into a blender. Add the ice cream and milk and blend until smooth.

LEFT **CARDAMOM, COFFEE, and DATE SHAKE**

RIGHT **VANILLA SUPREME**

LEFT STRAWBERRY and BALSAMIC MILKSHAKE

RIGHT SPICED PISTACHIO BUTTERMILK SHAKE

STRAWBERRY and BALSAMIC MILKSHAKE

Balsamic vinegar shows just how versatile an ingredient it is in this shake, bringing out the flavor of the strawberries perfectly. It also adds a refreshing tang to the creaminess of the milk.

Hull the strawberries and put in a blender with the balsamic vinegar, milk, and sorbet. Blend until smooth.

2 cups strawberries

1½–2 teaspoons balsamic vinegar

2 cups organic milk

4 scoops strawberry sorbet

SERVES: 4

PURPLE PUNCH SMOOTHIE

This thick purple drink is packed full of the goodness of the dark berries. You can use any single or mixed berry sorbet for this, depending on what is available. Alternatively, use a low-fat berry ice cream.

Put all the ingredients in a blender and blend until smooth.

¾ cup fresh or frozen blackberries

1 cup fresh or frozen blueberries

2 cups organic skimmed milk

2 scoops berry sorbet

SERVES: 4

SPICED PISTACHIO BUTTERMILK SHAKE

Pistachio nuts are a good source of fiber, vitamin B6, magnesium, potassium, and monounsaturated fat. The buttermilk cuts through the fat with a pleasant acidity, while the spices aid digestion of the other ingredients as well as offering a wonderfully aromatic flavor.

Peel and slice the banana. Put all the ingredients except the honey in a blender and blend until smooth. Add a teaspoon of honey if you find the buttermilk too tangy.

1 large banana

⅓ cup shelled unsalted pistachio nuts

¼ teaspoon apple pie spice

2 cups buttermilk

1 teaspoon honey, to taste

SERVES: 2

STRAWBERRY BUTTERMILK LASSI

Lassi is a South Asian drink originating from the Punjab region of India. Traditionally lassis were made by blending yogurt with spices, water, and salt until frothy and were often flavored with cumin. The sweet lassi is a more recent invention and is flavored with fruits such as strawberries or mangoes, or aromatics like rosewater. They are particularly refreshing and can be made with yogurt as well as buttermilk, as this one is.

Hull the strawberries and put them in a blender with the buttermilk and ice cubes. Blend until smooth. Check the taste and add 2 teaspoons of honey, if you like.

4 cups strawberries

2 cups buttermilk

8 ice cubes

2 teaspoons honey, to taste

SERVES: 2–3

ALMOND LASSI

Almond and rosewater make an aromatic and exotic drink—very refreshing on a hot summer's day served over ice. Magnesium and other minerals are found in almonds, and the combination of almonds and rosewater in this lassi aids in calming the nerves and muscles.

Put all the ingredients in a blender and blend until smooth.

Rosewater is uplifting, a stress reliever, and calms the nerves.

⅓ cup blanched almonds

1 tablespoon rosewater

2 teaspoons brown sugar

1¼ cups organic yogurt

6 ice cubes

SERVES: 1–2

ALMOND LASSI

STRAWBERRY FRUCHE

A fresh-tasting shake made with fromage frais (also known as fromage blanc), a fresh, soft cheese. Pure fromage frais is virtually fat free but often contains added cream, so check the label if you are cutting down on fat. If you can't find fromage frais, use fresh farmer cheese or Greek yogurt.

Hull the strawberries and put them in a blender with the fromage frais, cinnamon, and milk and blend until smooth. Serve topped with strawberry slices and a sprinkling of cinnamon.

2 cups strawberries, plus extra sliced strawberries to serve

8 oz. natural fromage frais

1 teaspoon ground cinnamon, plus extra to serve

1¼ cups organic milk

SERVES: 2

FROZEN BERRY SMOOTHIE

Frozen berries are great for blended drinks as they are available year round and can be blended straight from the freezer, making the drink thick and instantly chilled. This is a great one for kids—how many do you know who don't like berries and ice cream?

Put all the ingredients in a blender and blend until smooth.

1¼ cups frozen mixed berries

2 scoops vanilla ice cream

2 cups organic milk

SERVES: 2

MAPLE CUSTARD SHAKE

The custard apple or cherimoya, sometimes referred to as bullock's heart due to its shape, is a native of the Caribbean. The knobbly skin ranges in color from yellow to sage green to speckled brown when ripe. Inside, the flesh is cream with hidden black seeds, which should be discarded. The flavor, a cross between mango and banana, has a hint of custard about it, hence the name. In nutrition terms this fruit has it all—vitamins, minerals, proteins, and fiber. Its sweet creamy flesh will satisfy any hunger pangs and sustain energy levels between meals.

Cut the custard apple in half and scoop out the flesh, being careful to remove and discard all the seeds. Put the flesh in a blender with the remaining ingredients and blend until smooth.

1 custard apple (cherimoya), about 12 oz.

1 tablespoon pure maple syrup

2 scoops vanilla ice cream

2 cups organic milk

SERVES: 3

ABOVE **FROZEN BERRY SMOOTHIE**

BELOW **STRAWBERRY FRUCHE**

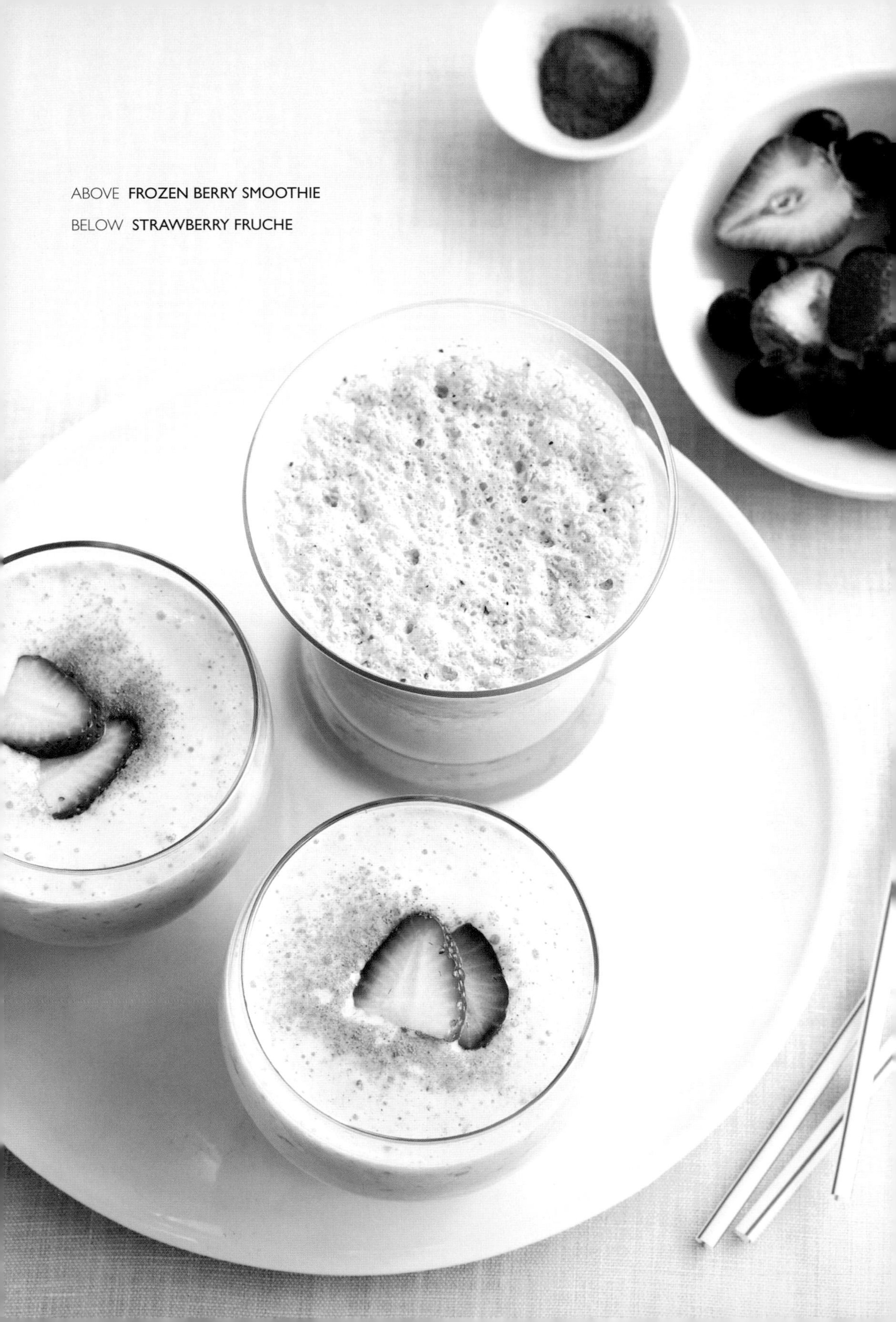

LEFT **MALTED CARAMEL SHAKE**
CENTER **SPICED COCONUT LASSI**
RIGHT **CHOCOLATE MILKSHAKE**

SPICED COCONUT LASSI

1⅔ cups coconut milk

1 cup organic milk

1 tablespoon honey

1 teaspoon apple pie spice

6 ice cubes

SERVES: 4

This spiced lassi enriched with coconut milk has a distinctive taste—creamy yet a little sharp, with the warmth of the spices. It is a nourishing drink and provides ongoing energy. The spices will help you digest the yogurt and coconut milk.

Put all the ingredients in a blender and blend until smooth.

CHOCOLATE MILKSHAKE

2 cups organic milk

1 tablespoon organic cocoa powder

4 scoops chocolate ice cream, plus extra to serve

SERVES: 2–3

This is a classic shake that reminds me of childhood summer milkshakes by the beach, served in tall aluminium glasses with a colored straw, ice-cold and totally delicious. As this version uses organic cocoa powder, it has the added advantage of being packed full of antioxidants. Buy a good-quality chocolate ice cream—the higher the cocoa-fat percentage, the better (check the label).

Put all the ingredients in a blender and blend until smooth. Serve in tall glasses with extra ice cream.

Organic cocoa powder is 14 times richer in antioxidants and flavonoids than red wine, 21 times more than green tea, and 7 times more than dark chocolate that is cold pressed without solvents and kept below 100°F. Phenylethylamine (PEA), found in cocoa products, is a chemical created in the brain when we fall in love; it also helps increase focus and alertness.

MALTED CARAMEL SHAKE

2 cups organic milk

2 tablespoons caramel sauce, plus extra to serve

2 tablespoons malted milk powder

2 scoops vanilla ice cream

SERVES: 2

This rich caramel-flavored shake is as much of a trip down memory lane as the Chocolate Milkshake. When I was a child, we used to whisk milk into a packet of powder mix called Angel Delight or Instant Whip, and I always chose the caramel one. This shake contains malted milk powder to give it that extra-thick malt flavor.

Put all the ingredients in a blender and blend until smooth. Serve in tall glasses, drizzled with a little extra caramel sauce.

DAIRY-FREE SMOOTHIES

Some smoothies and most shakes are made with milk or yogurt, but there are plenty of delicious non-dairy options for those who cannot, or prefer not to, consume dairy products. These alternatives include soy milk, rice milk, oat milk, and fruit juices. Dairy yogurt is often more tolerable than milk, but sheep's milk, goat's milk, and soy milk yogurts are available too. Sheep's milk and sheep's milk yogurt are both far higher in calcium than cow's milk, so are a great choice if you have an allergy to cow's milk. Goat's milk products are the most digestible of all milks and yogurts.

LEFT PINEAPPLE and PASSION FRUIT SOY SHAKE
RIGHT SOY, SESAME, and MAPLE SYRUP SMOOTHIE

SOY, SESAME, and MAPLE SYRUP SMOOTHIE

1 banana

2 tablespoons tahini

2 tablespoons pure maple syrup

1¼ cups soy milk

1 cup soy yogurt

SERVES: 2

You may find the inclusion of a savory ingredient such as tahini (sesame seed paste) strange in a smoothie, but it makes a delicious drink. Tahini helps boost calcium levels.

Peel and slice the banana and put it in a blender with the remaining ingredients. Blend until smooth.

When you buy soy milk, always read the label. Many of the nutrients in soy are destroyed during processing into milk, so most manufacturers fortify their products with additional vitamins such as B12 as well as calcium. Buy genetically modified organism-free, organic soy milk with no added malt, sugar, sweeteners, or vegetable oils. Soy mik contains little saturated fat.

DATE, BANANA, and RICE MILKSHAKE

4 Medjool dates, pitted

½ cup apple juice

2 bananas

1¼ cups rice milk

SERVES: 2

Dates provide a quick energy boost and satisfy sugar cravings. Choose plump, soft dates such as the Medjool variety, which give the shake a delicious caramel flavor. Avoid this drink if you suffer from hypoglycemia as the sugar high will be excessive, followed by a sugar low. Drink this before a run or other aerobic activity.

Put the dates and apple juice in a small saucepan, heat gently until boiling, then cover and simmer for 5 minutes until the dates are softened. Let cool completely.

Transfer the dates and juice to a blender. Peel and slice the bananas, add them and the rice milk to the blender, and blend until smooth.

Look for rice milk made from whole brown rice with no added rice or vegetable oils, salt, sugar, or sweeteners. Buy an organic brand if possible. Rice milk is best used chilled for maximum flavor.

PINEAPPLE and PASSION FRUIT SOY SHAKE

½ pineapple

½ cup passion fruit pulp

1 cup soy milk

4 scoops vanilla soy ice cream

SERVES: 3

A delicious combination of tropical fruit flavors. When choosing a pineapple, pull one of the outside leaves; if ripe, they will pull away easily. The more wrinkled a passion fruit, the riper its flesh. About 8 large passion fruit will yield ½ cup of pulp. Passion fruit pulp is also available in cans from large supermarkets.

Peel the pineapple, discard the tough central core, and chop the flesh. Put it in a blender with the passion fruit pulp, soy milk, and ice cream. Blend until smooth.

SPICED MANGO, COCONUT, and LIME SMOOTHIE

1 cup freshly brewed espresso
coffee

2 tablespoons malt extract

2 cups soy milk

3 scoops vanilla soy ice cream

ice cubes, to serve

SERVES: 3–4

MALTED COFFEE FRAPPÉ

Malt extract adds a delightfully nutty flavor to this drink, which is great served at breakfast time.

Make the coffee and while it is hot stir in the malt extract until dissolved. Set aside to cool completely. Transfer to a blender and add the milk and ice cream. Blend until smooth and serve over ice.

Malt extract is a natural sugar and is recognized as a great energy source.

1 banana

2 cups strawberries

2 tablespoons oat bran

2 cups oat milk

1 tablespoon malt extract

SERVES: 2

MALTED STRAWBERRY OAT SHAKE

This power-packed shake is great for kick-starting the day. Oat bran, eaten regularly, can help reduce your cholesterol levels by up to 25%. It adds a delicate nutty flavor and bulk to drinks.

Peel and slice the banana. Hull the strawberries and put them and the banana in a blender. Add the oat bran, oat milk, and malt extract and blend until smooth.

1 large mango, about 20 oz.

1⅔ cups coconut milk

freshly squeezed juice
of 1 lime

1 cup freshly squeezed
orange juice

½ teaspoon ground allspice

SERVES: 4

SPICED MANGO, COCONUT, and LIME SMOOTHIE

A delicious blend of flavors, and a nutritious and tasty drink.

To prepare the mango, slice down each side of the pit, and cut away the flesh from the skin. Put the flesh in a blender with the coconut milk, lime juice, orange juice, and allspice and blend until smooth.

Much has been written about coconut milk being bad for you because it is high in fat, but in fact its high levels of lauric acid (see page 7) will help you lose or maintain weight, reduce the risk of heart disease, and lower your cholesterol. It can also help those with diabetes and chronic fatigue, and improve irritable bowel syndrome and other digestive disorders. Coconut milk, with its antibacterial, antiviral, and antifungal agents, can prevent other illnesses, increase your metabolism, and promote healthy thyroid function. Finally, it will rejuvenate your skin and prevent wrinkles.

CARIBBEAN CRUISE

½ pineapple
1 small papaya, about 16 oz.
1¼ cups coconut milk
8 ice cubes

SERVES: 4

This smoothie is a stomach restorative, with potent enzymes found in both pineapple and papaya, and the antimicrobial properties of coconut milk. It is nutrient-dense to pick you up between meals, especially when you are craving sugar or hit an afternoon energy slump.

Peel the pineapple and discard the thick central core. Cut the flesh into chunks. Peel and halve the papaya, scoop out and discard the seeds, and chop the flesh. Put the pineapple and papaya in a blender, add the coconut milk and ice cubes, and blend until smooth.

Papaya contains papain, an enzyme that helps digest proteins, so it is an excellent digestive aid.

CREAMY BERRY SOY SHAKE

1 cup fresh or frozen raspberries
¾ cup fresh or frozen blackberries
2 scoops vanilla soy ice cream
2 cups soy milk

SERVES: 2–3

This is a thick, crazy colored, and totally delicious fruit drink that is ideal for children with dairy allergies. They will love the combination of ice cream and berries. You could substitute berry sorbet for the soy ice cream if you are finding it hard to locate.

Put all the ingredients in a blender and blend until smooth.

PEANUT and CAROB PROTEIN SMOOTHIE

2 bananas
8 oz. silken tofu
3 tablespoons smooth natural peanut butter
1 tablespoon honey
2 teaspoons carob powder
1¼ cups soy milk

SERVES: 2

A thick, heavy smoothie best chewed while drinking to help digestion of the ingredients. It is very filling and provides a healthy snack or a meal in itself. Carob is a chocolate alternative available from health-food stores.

Peel and slice the bananas and put in a blender. Add the remaining ingredients and blend until smooth.

Carob is produced from the ground seeds and pods of the carob tree. It does not contain caffeine as chocolate does and is high in fiber and calcium.

LEFT **CARIBBEAN CRUISE**

CENTER **CREAMY BERRY SOY SHAKE**

RIGHT **PEANUT and CAROB PROTEIN SMOOTHIE**

STRAWBERRY SOY SHAKE

2 cups strawberries

2 cups soy milk

4 scoops strawberry soy ice cream, plus extra to serve (optional)

SERVES: 2–3

A lovely summer drink when strawberries are at their sweet juicy best. If strawberries aren't in season, this shake works well with frozen berries too.

Hull the strawberries. Put all the ingredients in a blender and blend until smooth. Serve with an extra scoop of ice cream, if you like.

Strawberries are well known for their high nutritional value, but you may not know that they are also high in folic acid (folate). Folate is a water-soluble B vitamin that helps prevent birth defects such as spina bifida. It also helps the body absorb iron.

GREEN TEA DETOX

1 banana

2 teaspoons green tea powder

2 cups pear juice

1 teaspoon honey, to taste

SERVES: 2

Green tea is a powerful antioxidant. The Chinese and Japanese have used green tea as a medicine for centuries to help treat headaches and poor digestion, improve wellbeing, and extend life expectancy. Its health benefits include preventing cancer, reducing blood pressure, lowering cholesterol, strengthening bones, and nourishing the skin. It is also antibacterial and antiviral. Green tea powder is available from Asian shops and health-food stores.

Peel and slice the banana and put it in a blender with the green tea powder and pear juice. Blend until smooth. Add honey to taste, if preferred.

CHERRY BERRY CRUSH

2¼ cups frozen pitted cherries

1 cup frozen raspberries

1 tablespoon brown sugar

SERVES: 2

Super-rich in vitamin C, this is a great iron tonic. Cherries are much higher in vitamin C than citrus fruits and other berries, so this drink is also an excellent cold cure. If you can't find frozen cherries, use bottled cherries in natural syrup.

Put all the ingredients in a blender and blend until really smooth.

CHERRY BERRY CRUSH

CAROB and MAPLE
RICE MILK SHAKE

2 cups rice milk

2 tablespoons pure maple syrup

½ tablespoon carob powder

4 scoops chocolate soy ice cream

SERVES: 2

CAROB and MAPLE RICE MILK SHAKE

Carob has quite a strong flavor that can be overpowering, but the addition of maple syrup helps balance the flavors and imparts a lovely caramel taste to this drink. You can use organic cocoa powder instead of the carob powder, if you prefer.

Put all the ingredients in a blender and blend until smooth.

2 bananas

⅓ cup granola, plus extra to serve

2 cups soy milk

½ cup soy yogurt

1 teaspoon ground cinnamon, plus extra to serve

honey, to serve

SERVES: 2–3

BANANA and GRANOLA SOY SMOOTHIE

This is one of my favorite breakfast smoothies. I love the flavors of the sweet, nutty granola (which can be high in sugar, so check package labels) combined with the warm spiciness of the ground cinnamon.

Peel and slice the bananas. Put in a blender with the granola, soy milk, yogurt, and cinnamon and blend until smooth. Pour into glasses and serve topped with a little extra ground cinnamon, a sprinkling of granola, and a drizzle of honey.

LOW-FAT SMOOTHIES

By their nature most of the recipes in this book are good for you (and even the indulgent recipes are good for your soul!), but if you want to cut down on fat, try some of the wonderful combinations in this chapter. Many of the drinks are diluted with fruit juice rather than milk, and in some cases just the fruit is sufficient.

RASPBERRY, APPLE, and LYCHEE JUICE

2 oranges

1 lime

1 cup guava nectar

ice cubes, to serve

SERVES: 2

ORANGE, GUAVA, and LIME REFRESHER

A potent vitamin C drink; guava is particularly high in vitamin C, which is not only a tonic for your immune system but acts as a stress reliever. Excellent for recurrent infections anywhere in the body, guava nectar is available from most supermarkets and specialist food stores. Buy an unsweetened brand if possible.

Peel and chop the oranges and lime. Press the flesh through a juicer into a pitcher. Stir in the guava nectar. Half-fill 2 glasses with ice and top up with the juice.

1⅓ cups frozen raspberries

22 oz. canned lychees, drained

1 cup apple juice

SERVES: 2

RASPBERRY, APPLE, and LYCHEE JUICE

Like all berries, raspberries are a valuable source of antioxidants. I recommend frozen raspberries for juices, because if a raspberry is at its peak you really just want to pop it into your mouth and enjoy it neat! Many fresh raspberries are rather disappointing, and frozen raspberries are far cheaper too. Lychee juice is traditionally used to alleviate a cough and ulcers in the stomach. Use lychees in natural juice if you can find them.

Put all the ingredients in a blender and blend until smooth.

2 apples

4 pears

2-inch piece fresh ginger

ice cubes, to serve

SERVES: 2

PEAR, APPLE, and GINGER TINGLER

The tingle comes from the ginger, always a refreshing addition to juices. Pears reduce acidity and are one of the least allergenic of all fruits. The ginger combined with the fiber of the pears and apples moves congestion out of the body.

Roughly slice the apples and pears so they will fit into your juicer funnel. Press the apples, pears, and ginger through the juicer into a pitcher. Serve over ice.

LEFT **RHUBARB, YOGURT, and ROSEWATER SMOOTHIE**

RIGHT **GO GREEN JUICE**

RHUBARB, YOGURT, and ROSEWATER SMOOTHIE

6½ oz. trimmed rhubarb

3 tablespoons honey

1 cup organic low-fat yogurt

1 cup organic skim milk

1 tablespoon rosewater

SERVES: 2

This drink is almost thick enough to pour into a glass, chill, and serve as dessert; it is certainly tasty enough. As always, rosewater adds a hint of the exotic and will have people guessing.

Cut the rhubarb into 2-inch lengths and put in a saucepan with 2 tablespoons water and the honey. Bring slowly to a boil and simmer gently for 5–8 minutes until softened. Set aside until completely cold.

Put the cooled rhubarb mixture in a blender with the remaining ingredients and blend until smooth.

Rhubarb is a natural laxative and should be avoided if you have diarrhea. It is strongly astringent, which is evident from its tart flavor. Astringents strengthen mucous membranes, making them less susceptible to irritants and allergens.

GO GREEN JUICE

½ honeydew melon

2 kiwi fruit

6½ oz. grapes

¼ bunch mint sprigs (optional)

ice cubes, to serve

SERVES: 2

When choosing melons always smell them; a ripe melon's scent is heady and aromatic. Melon is a great diuretic and high in vitamin C. Grapes are also very cleansing—they are alkaline and highly nutritious—and kiwi fruit are packed with essential minerals, especially potassium. This good-for-you juice tastes sensational.

Peel and seed the melon, peel the kiwis, roughly chop all the flesh, and put in a blender. Add the grapes and the leaves picked from the mint sprigs, if using, and blend until really smooth. Serve over ice in highball glasses.

PEAR, BANANA, CARDAMOM, and YOGURT SMOOTHIE

2 bananas

2 cups organic pear juice

1 teaspoon ground cardamom

1 cup organic low-fat yogurt

SERVES: 2–3

Pear and cardamom are a great combination and with banana added the smoothie is thick and spicy—really yummy. This drink is an excellent tonic for an inflamed and over-acidic stomach. Cardamom is a digestive aid and organic yogurt, with its probiotics, helps balance the bacteria in your digestive system.

Peel and slice the bananas and put in a blender. Add the remaining ingredients and blend until smooth.

Cardamom is a heady spice that improves digestion and provides a seductive, aphrodisiac aroma. It was found in old-fashioned Arabian love potions.

PINEAPPLE, LIME, and YOGURT SHAKE

A tangy, aromatic shake that is both refreshing and delicious. It also has soothing qualities to calm an acidic stomach.

Peel the pineapple, discard the thick central core, and chop the flesh. Put it in a blender with the remaining ingredients and blend until smooth.

½ medium pineapple

freshly squeezed juice of 1 lime

1⅓ cups organic low-fat yogurt

SERVES: 2

SPICED MELON FROTHY

Melon and ginger are perfect partners in this refreshing shake. Orange-fleshed melons such as cantaloupes are a good source of beta-carotene as well as vitamin C.

Seed the melon and scoop the flesh into a blender. Add the ginger and pear juice and blend until smooth. Serve over ice.

2 lb. cantaloupe or other orange-fleshed melon

1-inch piece fresh ginger, peeled

1 cup pear juice

ice cubes, to serve

SERVES: 2–3

BERRY BOOST

This colorful thick juice is a boost indeed, packed full of vitamin C, antioxidants, and bioflavonoids. Cranberry juice is great for urinary-tract infections such as cystitis, but beware of added sugars. If you can find fresh cranberries, add a handful to the blender and complete the recipe with 1 cup apple juice instead of the cranberry juice.

Put all the ingredients in a blender and blend until smooth.

1 cup frozen blueberries

1 cup frozen raspberries

1 cup frozen strawberries

1 cup cranberry juice

SERVES: 2–3

RASPBERRY, VANILLA, and BUTTERMILK FROTH

2 cups frozen raspberries

1 teaspoon pure vanilla extract

2½ cups buttermilk

1–2 tablespoons brown sugar, to taste

SERVES: 2–3

Buttermilk has a similar flavor to yogurt and it is low in saturated fat. The combination of vanilla, raspberry, and buttermilk in this drink is subtle and unusual.

Put the raspberries, vanilla extract, and buttermilk in a blender and blend until smooth. Check the taste and add 1–2 tablespoons sugar, if you like.

STRAWBERRY, PEAR, and YAKULT SHAKE

4 cups strawberries

2 cups pear juice

2 scoops low-fat frozen strawberry yogurt

2 bottles Yakult

SERVES: 2–3

Yakult is a Japanese citrus-flavored, yogurt-like drink made by fermenting a mixture of skimmed milk and sugar with a strain of bacteria, *Lactobacillus casei*, that is naturally found in the digestive system. Yakult is believed to be beneficial for intestinal health and is available at many whole-foods stores. This would be an ideal shake to drink when you are taking a course of antibiotics.

Hull the strawberries and put them in a blender with the remaining ingredients. Blend until smooth.

TROPICAL FRUIT FEAST

1 large mango, about 1¼ lb.

½ pineapple

½ cup passion fruit pulp

1 cup guava nectar

SERVES: 2

A blend of the best exotic fruits in a glass—choose the mango with the headiest aroma, the sweetest pineapple, and the most wrinkled passion fruit and you will have a wonderfully refreshing tropical treat. The uplifting properties of these nutrient-dense fruits are great for your vitality and libido. About 4 large fresh passion fruit will yield ½ cup of pulp, or you can buy it in a can.

To prepare the mango, slice down each side of the pit and cut away the flesh from the skin. Put the flesh in a blender. Peel the pineapple, discard the thick central core, and chop the flesh. Add to the blender with the remaining ingredients and blend until smooth.

CLOCKWISE FROM LEFT **TROPICAL FRUIT FEAST;**

STRAWBERRY, PEAR, and YAKULT SHAKE;

RASPBERRY, VANILLA, and BUTTERMILK FROTH

BANANA, NUTMEG, and
HONEY SMOOTHIE

2 bananas

1 teaspoon honey

2 tablespoons oat bran

2 tablespoons raisins

1 cup organic skim milk

1 cup organic low-fat yogurt

¼ teaspoon freshly grated
nutmeg, plus extra to dust

SERVES: 2

BANANA, NUTMEG,
and HONEY SMOOTHIE

This is breakfast in a glass. Bananas add bulk as well as providing us with energy, oat bran helps reduce cholesterol levels, and raisins are an antioxidant-rich fruit and instant energy source. The nutmeg adds a touch of spice and aids digestion and appetite. It also alleviates nausea and vomiting.

Peel and slice the bananas. Put them in a blender with the remaining ingredients and blend until smooth. Serve dusted with a little extra grated nutmeg.

1¼ cups frozen blueberries

1 cup organic skim milk

2 scoops frozen vanilla yogurt

1 tablespoon honey

SERVES: 2

PURPLE THICKSHAKE

Blueberries, apart from their high antioxidant count, are a great blood cleanser and are also indicated for skin health. If you haven't got any blueberries in the freezer, you could use frozen raspberries, frozen strawberries, or a mixture of frozen berries as an alternative—they all make a delicious and healthy shake.

Put all the ingredients in a blender and blend until smooth.

4 apples

2 cups strawberries

1-inch piece fresh ginger

1 cup apricot nectar

ice cubes, to serve

SERVES: 2

STRAWBERRY, APPLE,
APRICOT, and GINGER JUICE

A refreshing drink with a hit of spice from the ginger. You can use pears instead of apples if you prefer, or a combination of both. Buy unsweetened apricot nectar without preservatives, if possible.

Cut the apples into chunks and hull the strawberries. Press the apples, strawberries, and ginger through a juicer into a pitcher and stir in the apricot nectar. Half-fill 2 highball glasses with ice and pour the juice over to serve.

ORANGE SUNSET

Reminiscent of the classic cocktail Tequila Sunrise but without the alcohol, this tangy juice is a vibrant orange with a hint of fiery red as the pomegranate juice sinks to the bottom of the glass. This drink is an immunity-building tonic to prevent colds and flu.

6 oranges
2 pomegranates

SERVES: 2

Peel the oranges, chop, and press through a juicer into a pitcher. Halve the pomegranates and, using a citrus juicer, squeeze the juice into a separate pitcher.

Pour the orange juice into 2 tumblers then pour in the pomegranate juice in a thin stream. Serve immediately.

Pomegranates are high in vitamin C and potassium and are a good source of fiber. Pomegranate juice is high in three different types of polyphenols (potent antioxidants): tannin, anthocyanin, and ellagic acid. Recent studies have found these substances help delay the onset of Alzheimer's.

STRAWBERRY and CRANAPPLE CRUSH

I often use crisp green-skinned apples such as Granny Smiths for juices. The color is pretty and I find they yield more juice than some softer varieties. The high apple content in this drink makes it an excellent source of pectin, a soluble fiber that soothes the intestines and moves the bowels. Cranberry is also a cleanser, for the urinary tract.

4 apples
2½ cups strawberries
1 cup cranberry juice
ice cubes, to serve

SERVES: 2

Chop the apples into chunks and hull the strawberries. Press the apple pieces and strawberries through a juicer into a pitcher and stir in the cranberry juice. Half-fill 2 large glasses with ice, add the juice, and serve.

WATERMELON and PEAR FROTHY

I was never a huge watermelon fan until I concocted this drink, but it is so delicious that it may well be my favorite in the book. The combination of thin fragrant watermelon juice and the thick, almost chalky pear juice is perfect. This is a cooling drink and therefore very beneficial for hot flushes and fever.

3 pears
1¼-lb. wedge watermelon
ice cubes, to serve

SERVES: 2–3

Cut the pears into pieces small enough to fit through the funnel of your juicer and press through into a pitcher. Cut the watermelon flesh into chunks. Put it in a blender with the pear juice and blend until smooth. Serve over ice.

INDULGENT SMOOTHIES

There are times when we all need a treat. What could be better than a delicious glass or mug of your favorite drink? This final chapter is all about indulgence, and whether it's the ripest of fruit blended with a rich ice cream or dark chocolate warmed with mint-infused milk, topped with a swirl of whipped cream, it's all about quality. It's good to be wicked once in a while. Enjoy.

2 cups strawberries, plus extra
sliced strawberries to serve

1 cup organic milk

½ cup Greek yogurt

2 scoops strawberry ice
cream, plus extra to serve

1 tablespoon strawberry syrup

SERVES: 2

STRAWBERRY EXTRAVAGANZA

A wonderfully indulgent drink guaranteed to delight the senses
—it's as pretty as it is delicious. Many brands of strawberry syrup
taste quite artificial, so try and find a more natural syrup from a
specialist food store or delicatessen.

Hull the strawberries and put them in a blender with the milk, yogurt, and ice
cream and blend until smooth.

Drizzle the strawberry syrup around the inside edges of 2 highball glasses, so it
can dribble down inside. Pour in the drink and serve with an extra scoop of ice
cream and sliced strawberries on top.

2 peaches

1 teaspoon brown sugar

1 cup organic milk

2 scoops vanilla ice cream

SERVES: 2

ROASTED PEACHES and CREAM

Roasting the peaches adds a sweet, caramel flavor to this
drink and is a great idea if the peaches are slightly underripe.
I prefer to use orange-fleshed, freestone peaches for color and
convenience, as the pits are easier to remove than those of
clingstone varieties, but any type of peach will work.

Preheat the oven to 375°F (190°C). Cut the peaches in half and discard the pits.
Arrange the peach halves cut side up in a foil-lined roasting pan and sprinkle over
the sugar. Bake for 20–25 minutes until the peaches are tender, remove from the
oven, and set aside until cold.

Chop the peaches, transfer to a blender, add the remaining ingredients, and blend
until smooth.

2 cups organic milk

4 sprigs of mint

3½ oz. bittersweet chocolate,
finely chopped

1 teaspoon sugar

½ cup whipped cream

SERVES: 2

WARM CHOCOLATE and MINT CREAM

This is the prefect drink for a chilly winter's evening—sweet
and chocolatey with a wonderful mint flavor. If you prefer your
chocolate mint-free, just omit the mint sprigs.

Put the milk and mint sprigs in a saucepan and bring to a boil over low heat. As
soon as the milk boils, remove the pan from the heat and let infuse for 15 minutes.

Discard the mint sprigs and reheat the milk to boiling point. Remove the pan from
the heat and stir in the chocolate and sugar until melted. Transfer to a blender
and blend until frothy. Pour into 2 mugs and spoon over the whipped cream.

CLOCKWISE FROM LEFT

PEANUT MAPLE CRUNCH,

MOCHA ICE CREAM SPECIAL,

WHITE CHOCOLATE FROTHY

2 cups freshly brewed coffee

1½ oz. semisweet chocolate, finely chopped

1 cup organic milk

4 scoops vanilla ice cream

4 scoops chocolate ice cream

SERVES: 2

MOCHA ICE CREAM SPECIAL

Very thick, rich, and totally divine, this drink is simply delicious. Coffee and chocolate are perfect partners—earthy, aromatic, and satisfying. Use an organic, freshly roasted and ground coffee for an intense flavor and extra kick.

As soon as the coffee is made, transfer it to a pitcher and stir in the chocolate until melted. Set aside to cool.

Put the cold coffee in a blender with the milk and 2 scoops of each flavor ice cream. Blend until smooth. Add a scoop each of vanilla and chocolate ice cream to 2 tall glasses, pour over the drink, and serve.

2 cups organic milk

2 tablespoons crunchy peanut butter

1 tablespoon pure maple syrup

2 scoops vanilla ice cream, plus extra to serve

SERVES: 2

PEANUT MAPLE CRUNCH

If you're feeling in need of a mood booster, then try this fabulous combination of peanut butter, maple syrup, and ice cream. It is sweet and nutty and the perfect indulgence.

Put all the ingredients in a blender and blend until smooth. Serve topped with extra ice cream.

2½ cups organic milk

1½ oz. white chocolate, grated

sweetened cocoa powder, for sprinkling (optional)

ground cinnamon, for sprinkling (optional)

SERVES: 2

WHITE CHOCOLATE FROTHY

A luxurious steamed milk drink without the coffee kick. If you have a coffeemaker, use its steam element to foam the chocolate milk for a really frothy, almost cappuccino-like effect.

Warm 2 mugs or heatproof glasses. Heat the milk in a saucepan until it just reaches boiling point and then stir in the chocolate until melted. Froth the milk using a whisk, hand blender, or coffeemaker, and pour into the warmed mugs. Serve dusted with cocoa powder and ground cinnamon, if you like.

PEACH MELBA RIPPLE

To save a few minutes you can simply blend all the ingredients together in one go, but I like the rippled effect of swirling the peach and raspberry flavors together just before serving. Both taste equally good.

Put the peach halves, half the vanilla extract, half the milk, and 2 scoops of vanilla ice cream in a blender. Blend until smooth and divide between 2 or 3 tumblers. Repeat with the raspberries and remaining vanilla, milk, and ice cream. Drizzle the raspberry mixture carefully into the glasses to give a ripple effect.

4 canned peach halves in natural juice, drained

I teaspoon pure vanilla extract

2 cups organic milk

4 scoops vanilla ice cream

I cup raspberries

SERVES: 2–3

LEMON CHEESECAKE SHAKE

Sharp and tangy, this confection is just like cheesecake in a glass. If you serve it with graham crackers or ginger cookies, you almost have the real thing!

Put all the ingredients in a blender and blend until smooth.

3½ oz. cream cheese

grated zest and freshly squeezed juice of ½ unwaxed lemon

¼ cup prepared lemon curd

½ cup Greek yogurt

I cup organic milk

SERVES: 3–4

STRAWBERRY MERINGUE INDULGENCE

This is such a rich, indulgent drink it could be served as a summer dessert. For a more chunky texture—think gooey meringue—blend for just a short burst.

Put all the ingredients in a blender and blend until smooth.

2 cups strawberries or raspberries, or a mixture of both

2 meringues, about 2 oz.

½ cup light cream

I cup organic milk

I teaspoon pure vanilla extract

SERVES: 3–4

LEFT   PEACH MELBA RIPPLE

RIGHT   LEMON CHEESECAKE SHAKE

TURKISH DELIGHT FROTHY

This is a sweet indulgence with a hint of rosewater from the Turkish delight. Even after blending you will find small pieces of Turkish delight in the bottom of the glass—the best bits!

Put the milk and Turkish delight in a saucepan and heat very gently, stirring until the Turkish delight is half melted. Transfer to a blender and blend until frothy.

2 cups organic milk

1½ oz. rosewater-flavored Turkish delight (rahat loukoum), chopped

SERVES: 2

TRIPLE CHOCOLATE SHAKE

There are some days when nothing but chocolate will do the trick. If you're having one of those days, go for this shake.

Break the white chocolate into small pieces and put in a heatproof bowl set over a small saucepan of gently simmering water (do not let the bowl touch the water). Stir until melted. Dip the tops of 2 highball glasses into the chocolate and, using a teaspoon, drizzle the remaining chocolate down inside the glasses.

Put the dark chocolate, milk, and ice cream in a blender, blend until smooth, and pour into the glasses. Serve at once, sprinkled with a little grated chocolate.

1½ oz. white chocolate

1½ oz. semisweet chocolate, finely grated, plus extra to serve

2 cups organic milk

4 scoops chocolate ice cream

SERVES: 2

CHERRY TIRAMISÙ

Another dessert in a glass—this is truly indulgent and not for the faint-hearted, but it is the ultimate treat. (Tiramisù means "pick me up" in Italian.) Add Amaretto to make this a special after-dinner drink.

Put all the ingredients in a blender and blend until smooth. Serve sprinkled with grated chocolate.

1 oz. amaretti biscuits

1 cup pitted cherries, thawed if frozen

3½ oz. mascarpone

1 cup organic milk

1 tablespoon espresso coffee, chilled

1 tablespoon Amaretto liqueur (optional)

½ oz. semisweet chocolate, grated, to serve

SERVES: 2–3

INDEX